How To Find Your Soulmate

The Person You Thought Would Be Your Soul Mate May Not Be As Close As You Think. This Book Will Teach You How To Spot True Love And How To Spot Relationship Red Flags

Krzysztof Mitterer

TABLE OF CONTENT

Be vulnerable 1
Exhibit your capacity for understanding and genuine care towards them. 3
Please ensure that you possess genuine compatibility 26
Display your jovial demeanor to him. 52
Effective Communication Strategies: Establishing Effective Communication with Your Partner 93
Attracting Your Ideal Relationship 149

Be vulnerable

Nobody desires to engage in a romantic relationship with an individual who consistently strives to uphold a flawless appearance. If you are unable to uncover your imperfections, you will create an impression of being excessively perfect.

In order to discover romantic love, one must demonstrate openness by freely expressing their emotions and displaying vulnerability. I can guarantee that adopting a callous demeanor will not lead you to any positive outcomes.

Revealing one's less-than-perfect aspects can engender a deeper affection from others, as the desire for intimacy is inherent in human nature.

Additionally, ensure that there is a clear understanding that your trustworthiness can be relied upon.

Trust is a crucial element in interpersonal connections, and its absence undermines the longevity of love. To ascertain how to foster romantic affection in others, it is imperative that you establish a sense of trustworthiness and reliability.

Maintain confidentiality, exhibit integrity in your conduct, and strive for consistency between your words and deeds.

Exhibit your capacity for understanding and genuine care towards them.

This literary work concerning the techniques of inducing affection in another individual proves to be more challenging in practical application than initially anticipated. When I use the term "care," I am referring to the act of showing genuine concern for the well-being of others, demonstrating your appreciation for their presence and worth. When seeking romantic companionship, exhibiting a callous disposition is not a viable choice.

If you adopt an indifferent demeanor, you will inadvertently compel them to depart, leaving you with a sense of foolishness. Similarly, extend an invitation to individuals and ensure you are readily available to offer support when they require it.

Engage in the exploration of diverse expressions of love and discern which one resonates most with their preferences.

How to Foster Long-lasting Authentic Love" or "Strategies for Sustaining Genuine Love

Numerous explanations regarding the waning of love can be discovered through comprehending the mechanics and motivations behind the creation of an idealized emotional bond. The inhibition of one's imagination serves as the most significant impediment to cultivating love. Even after we have relinquished our defenses and embraced the experience of love, when fear creeps in, whether it be the fear of losing our partner or the fear of deviating from our accustomed sense of self, we may seek solace in a fantasy bond. This bond enables us to uphold the illusion of not being alone, all the while creating emotional detachment from our partner. In order to preempt the establishment of an illusionary association, it is advisable to not only steer clear of the aforementioned qualities, but also partake in the following pursuits.

Steps to dispel an imagined emotional connection and cultivate a deeper capacity for affection:

Display warmth: Seek out subtle means to engage in physical contact and express fondness and desire.

Adopt a slower pace and focus on the present moment. Allocate time for effective communication and active listening with your partner.

Maintain visual connection: Although it may appear effortless, it is common for us to overlook the simple act of briefly gazing at our conversational partner.

Consider attempting something that has been done in the past: Allocate time and perseveringly engage in activities that brought you both enjoyment before.

Seek novelty: Avoid the mere acquisition of routines. Continuously introduce novel pursuits and remain open to the ones suggested by your partner.

Deviate from the norm: If the monotony of repetition is dampening your enthusiasm, consider actively diverging from your habitual routine and embracing the possibilities of spontaneity.

Refrain from being passive and dominant: Aim for a fair and balanced exchange of viewpoints. Assume accountability for your actions and refrain from exerting dominance over your spouse.

Addressing the situation from an individual perspective is advised, rather than using a collective voice. It is imperative to acknowledge and respect the distinct identities within the dynamic, avoiding actions or behaviors that may diminish the level of mutual attraction.

Please remain conscious of your critical internal dialogue: Each of us possesses an internal nemesis that passes judgment on ourselves and our partner, thereby undermining our most intimate bonds.

Engage in autonomous activities: Merely being in a relationship does not necessitate participating in all pursuits collectively. It is advised not to forsake personal connections and activities that bring you joy, and it is equally important not to impose the same on your partner.

Express your emotions and thoughts effectively: Do not anticipate your spouse to possess telepathic abilities. Expressing your desires and emotions in a straightforward manner enables you to steer clear of employing passive-aggressive or abrasive approaches to communication. It also motivates your spouse to engage in similar behavior.

Do not engage in a mindset of reciprocal retaliation: Love is a conscious choice that each individual must make for themselves. By commencing the process of assigning measurable value to our actions towards one another, we develop anticipations and provoke feelings of bitterness, rather than remaining attuned to the profound sentiments associated with demonstrating affection for others.

Uphold the endeavors that bring joy to your spouse: Continuously provide encouragement and motivation to enable your spouse to flourish and pursue activities that truly resonate with their authentic self, even in instances where those pursuits may not hold the highest significance for you.

Engage in activities that your spouse perceives as acts of love: Ensure that the actions you take hold significance for your spouse. Do you hold a fondness for receiving floral arrangements, or would this gesture truly convey your affection to your spouse?

Do not adopt a state of emotional confinement: It is exceedingly facile to withdraw and detach ourselves when experiencing shame, fear, disappointment, or provocation from our partner. However, we must diligently strive to remain receptive and resist the inclination to reject the affection that is bestowed upon us.

Day five: Crafting your online dating profile.

After four days of our journey, you are now prepared to commence the composition of your meticulously crafted online dating profile. One of the predominant factors contributing to the failure of establishing connections among individuals lies in the presence of either an excessively ambiguous or inadequately completed profile.

Some individuals hastily register, but fail to complete critical text fields, resulting in disappointment for those who come across their profiles and click on them. It is highly unlikely that you will receive a reply if your profile is replete with statements such as, "I'll complete this section at a later time," or the exceptionally banal response: "I perpetually struggle to articulate things about myself." Equally detrimental, it must be noted, is expressing disdain for the process with statements like, "I despise completing these profiles," which reveals a sense of weariness born from extensive online dating experiences.

There may be instances where some individuals complete their profile by presenting a false or misleading image of themselves. What are the reasons for considering it an unfavorable notion? To begin with, it should be noted that even if you are projecting an idealized version of yourself, the individual whom other online daters establish a connection with will inevitably diverge as they draw closer to you. You may initially succeed in perpetuating this persona during early dates or online conversations, but eventually your true nature will be uncovered. Please provide an accurate and straightforward account of the situation.

Lastly, there are individuals among you who may unfortunately fall victim to the gravest transgression of all: the inability to discern their desired attributes in a prospective partner. This has been the underlying cause for our extensive efforts in diligently identifying the internal and external attributes of your preferred companion throughout the past few days.

Please collect your journals from the previous four days and make ready to establish your brand new profile.

The Exemplary Structure of an Ideal Online Dating Profile

Although each online dating platform may vary in their structure, the content of your messages should remain consistent, irrespective of any necessary adjustments in sequencing. There are three essential points that every online profile should emphasize:

Your core values
Your personality
The object of your search

Failure to include any of these important components in your online dating communication would result in you overlooking the chance to allure your ideal counterpart, consequently dissuading potential suitors who could otherwise be actively seeking your companionship.

Constructing Your Opening Hook

Similar to the guidance provided by your English educators, it is imperative to captivate the reader's attention in the initial sentences, for failing to do so will only result in causing tedium for those visiting your profile. You can achieve this by crafting a captivating introduction that not only showcases your individuality but also provides your potential partner with a glimpse into the type of person you are seeking.

As an illustration, I would like to refer to a profile that I personally developed and constructed in the past.

The notion of 'someday' constitutes an ailment that inflicts detrimental consequences on one's spirit and aspirations. Do not defer your aspirations to an uncertain future. Instead, cultivate ambitious dreams, harbor even greater beliefs, and always bear in mind that each of us has a unique path to traverse. Do not engage in comparisons with other individuals. If it brings about a sense of pleasure or contentment, proceed with the action. Wear your sunscreen. Engage in spontaneous acts of benevolence. That is the wisdom I have for you today.

Do you consider it rather trite? The magnitude of responses generated by this solitary paragraph is truly astounding. My email folder was inundated with compelling and thought-provoking responses. To derive inspiration, one may reflect upon adages, quotations from films, and other proverbial expressions that resonate with personal sensibilities. Begin the composition by formulating your introductory paragraph, subsequently proceeding to address the subsequent segment.

Describing the Authentic You

On the second day, our efforts were focused on the exploration of your true essence, where we endeavored to discern three to five inherent and manifest attributes that define your being. Locate the aforementioned exercise and utilize them to construct a concise written passage that integrates all of these characteristics, effectively articulating your essence to a global audience.

Subsequently, incorporate a selection of your preferred pastimes, delving into favored pursuits, literary works, films, music, and locales.

Once more, extracted from my personal profile, this is what I meticulously composed:

I am Brandon, an individual engaged in writing, entrepreneurial pursuits, and the realm of creativity. As an individual growing up, I encountered an inspiring display of my parents' resolute drive and unwavering determination in establishing their businesses. Consequently, I adopted that very same entrepreneurial mindset and fervor. I enjoy taking on leadership roles, while also being proficient in collaborative teamwork. ENTJ.

Depending on the circumstances of my week and personal agenda, I possess the tendency to stay at home, yet I derive pleasure from engaging in social outings with acquaintances over libations and delectable cuisine. My interests encompass the realms of theatre, politics, food trucks, bowling, reading (I possess an insatiable appetite for literature), engaging in writing both as a leisure activity and as a means of financial gain, as well as delving into the art of filmmaking.

Describing Your Perfect Match

On Day 4, we endeavored to discern your ideal counterpart through a process of discerning three to five core internal and external attributes that hold utmost significance to you in selecting a partner. Locate the aforementioned exercise and utilize its content to compose a paragraph or two elucidating your desired acquaintance.

Another illustration from my personal profile:

I am actively seeking a meaningful romantic relationship, with a focus on long-term commitment, and ultimately, my goal is to find a lifetime partner. A singular individual, bound by timelessness, to remain steadfastly by his side while being assured of his reciprocal fidelity. Any individual can engage in sexual activity, yet I aspire to exemplify the qualities of a mature gentleman who demonstrates an encompassing display of affection, dedication, and appreciation towards another person. I am desirous of establishing a profound connection and nurturing a familial bond.

I am unfamiliar with your identity at present. However, the individual in question possesses admirable ethical qualities, shows kindness, possesses an excellent sense of humor, and seeks stability over fleeting encounters and a lack of commitment. One ought to possess a consistent profession or, at the very least, a thoughtfully devised strategy outlining the means by which they shall attain their goals. Having dependable means of transportation is advantageous, nonetheless unforeseen circumstances can arise. Most importantly, this person values their family and will undoubtedly bring joy to my mother.

Refine your language until you feel at ease. Tomorrow, you're going live.

To whom do your signals intend to reach?
Upon all this discourse regarding signals, you might be inquisitive as to the recipients of these signals. The correct response is that it applies to all individuals. While you may not be intentionally engaging in flirtatious behavior with every person, it is still beneficial to present a genial and appealing demeanor to everyone you encounter. Demonstrating an attitude of

affability towards all individuals you encounter, even those unfamiliar to you, will effectively enhance your chances of expanding your social network, securing employment opportunities, and ultimately attracting a desirable partner.

Develop the habit of smiling at individuals indiscriminately, thereby ensuring your preparedness for the fortuitous occasion when an appropriate partner presents themselves. It is imperative that each individual engage in this activity, irrespective of self-perceived perfection. Every individual possesses a perfect match in the world. I will assist them in locating your whereabouts. It is evident that you are not obliged to reciprocate romantic affections towards every man who engages in conversational interaction with you. Nevertheless, every individual can derive advantage from occasional acts of benevolence and congeniality.

This concept holds significant significance when it comes to comprehending contemporary relationships and relinquishing the idealized notion of a flawless partner. In the realm of most fantasies, it is commonplace to witness the sudden enchanting emergence of an individual that possesses an impeccable disposition, capturing your attention and persuading your weary spirit that he is unequivocally the epitome of an ideal romantic partner, and your most ardent admirer.

In actuality, an ideal gentleman does not manifest inexplicably and ingratiate himself into your existence. There may be individuals of questionable character who could attempt to engage in such behavior, but it is important to note that the individual who is perfectly suited for you is currently occupied with their own endeavors and is respectful of maintaining boundaries within your personal sphere. Consequently, it holds great significance to grant a man, indeed all men, the permission to initiate a conversation. Have you ever pondered the reasons behind the seeming allure that some women possess, which invariably attracts the attention of many suitors? This is how!

The majority of men grapple with their own personal insecurities and are hesitant to approach an attractive woman unless they receive clear and persuasive indicators of interest. In essence, Prince Charming possesses the knowledge of precisely when to extend an invitation for a social engagement. In actuality, a virtuous gentleman demonstrates reverence for your personal boundaries and proceeds with prudence.

The majority of gentlemen do not spontaneously materialize in one's existence and insist on inviting one to a romantic dining experience. Those who intend to engage in such behavior often exhibit a particular demeanor and may carry certain burdens, therefore caution is advised. (We will further discuss personality types in 5)

Impression, Impression – Oh, the Initial Perception

The prevailing motif observed throughout this is that initial impressions hold significant weight. It is inherent in human nature for individuals to possess a tendency towards superficial judgments based on initial appearances. Upon obtaining the knowledge of a new friend or acquaintance's identity, do you not instinctively assign a particular categorization to this individual?

His name is Scott, and he is a highly skilled gymnast. His name is Michael and he works as a cashier at the store. Her name is Kay, and she is a professional ballet dancer. If one fails to promptly establish their own distinctive identity, those in their surroundings will inevitably construct an identity on their behalf.

Regrettably, individuals who display negligence may find that classifying a recent acquaintance can possess a sense of unkindness. He is George, the individual who engages in nasal excavation. That individual over there is Cynthia, the young lady who has inadvertently become a recipient of an embarrassing incident involving the attachment of toilet paper to her footwear. Once individuals become stigmatized with these labels, it proves exceedingly arduous to disassociate oneself from such perceptions. Why, in your perspective, did William Shatner encounter significant challenges in being regarded as a credible actor? Indeed, we designated him as Captain Kirk.

Although it is unjust to solely evaluate an individual based on their physical appearance, it remains an undeniable reality that human nature often leads us to form associations with others based on initial impressions. Although initial assessments can be subject to revision and reevaluation, it is unlikely that unfamiliar individuals will invest the effort to reassess their perception of you. They will ascertain an identifier, and you shall perpetually retain said identifier.

Hence, I urge unmarried women to acknowledge this fact and endeavor to consistently present themselves in an optimal manner, encompassing not only physical appearance but also demeanor and conduct. It is imperative to consistently project a positive and captivating image of oneself, adopting the notion that one is constantly under observation. (Probability suggests that if there is a male individual present within the premises, his attention might be directed towards you.)

Captivating a Gentleman's Interest in Any Environment" or "Enthralling the Attention of a Man in Any Situation
When you experience a sense of attractiveness (and put forth an intentional effort to convey attractiveness to those around you), you exhibit a stride that exudes self-assurance and elegance. This method is

optimal for garnering the attention of even the most remote individuals. One intriguing aspect of attraction is that it is not subjective to voluntary control. We have no control over our innate preferences, irrespective of our gender.

Moreover, the concept of attraction remains consistent irrespective of the setting in which one encounters an individual, be it a club, a bar, a shopping center, a supermarket, or even through digital platforms. When one establishes a favorable initial perception, the bond flourishes rapidly and the semblance of romantic attraction is effortlessly kindled.

Conversely, should you fail to create a positive initial impression, irrespective of the context, it becomes exceedingly challenging for others to regard you with credibility during subsequent encounters. Numerous unmarried ladies tend to excessively prioritize enhancing their attractiveness, often disregarding crucial elements of establishing a favorable initial perception. Appearance is not the sole determinant. In addition, it is not solely contingent upon external appearances.

A favorable initial impression is achieved through the symbiosis of exceptional attire, impeccable verbal adeptness, and remarkable self-regulation. What strategies can one employ to establish a positive initial impact that extends beyond mere physical appearance? Additionally, it is imperative to consider not only the significance of your personal conduct but also the significance of the interaction and dialogue you engage in with others.

Please ensure that you possess genuine compatibility

As your relationship progresses, ascertain his aspirations and goals for the future. What is his plan for implementing his goals? What measures will he undertake in order to attain those goals? Do his goals coincide with yours? The attainment of success is frequently foreseen through the alignment of collective objectives, principles, and experiences. Please refrain from disregarding substantial differences in opinion under the assumption that either party will eventually change their mind. This approach, characterized by its high volatility and lack of realism, may ultimately result in prolonged disappointment.

Furthermore, obtaining a college degree provides a relatively dependable measure of achievement. The divorce rates among individuals who pursue higher education and postpone marriage until after completing college show a notable decrease compared to the approximately 50% average observed nationwide. Avoid rushing into a long-term commitment by postponing your education or permitting your spouse to postpone theirs. It is common for individuals to determine compatibility based on predetermined and structured factors, such as having similar personalities, shared interests, or common hobbies.

Nevertheless, should excessive significance be attributed to these factors, one may develop a belief that one is powerless in the face of adversity. One can easily become entangled in the thought pattern of believing, "There exists no purpose in making an effort due to our profound differences." Individuals' behaviors are not predestined and easily foreseen. Each individual undergoes a continual process of personal development, transformation, and, ideally, acquisition of knowledge. The amount of time you allocate to each other, the willingness of both parties to give and receive, and the shared aspiration to collaborate all contribute to the level of compatibility between you.

Naturally, an initial commonality greatly assists, albeit one that is more likely to encompass fundamental aspects such as shared values, perspectives, and ideologies - elements of genuine importance. Moreover, it is essential to continuously nurture every relationship to sustain its vitality. In case you harbor any concerns regarding the compatibility of you and your partner, our quiz can provide valuable assistance. It will afford you the opportunity to evaluate the compatibility of your shared values, assess the extent of your efforts invested in fostering and sustaining that compatibility, and determine actionable steps for its growth.

How would you define compatibility within the context of a relationship?

Primarily, when a couple engages in interactions characterized by respect and egalitarianism, their relationship demonstrates compatibility. Couples should derive pleasure from their shared experiences and engage in recreational activities together. Robust and fruitful relationships ensue when two individuals partake in mutual companionship and engage in shared activities. However, it is not necessary for a couple to possess identical interests.

Numerous individuals succumb to the fallacy that there exists a singular individual capable of fulfilling their every aspect, or serving as their "soulmate." This mindset can lead them to dismiss potential partners who do not conform to their idealized vision of an ideal spouse. Even if one does encounter a person who closely aligns with their preferences, it is improbable that this individual will perfectly coincide with all of their interests and fulfill every requirement. Furthermore, cultivating friendships enables one to establish a broader network of support and companionship, consequently facilitating one's holistic personal growth.

Given that no individual is exempt from imperfections, it is inevitable for any form of partnership to encounter challenges. Nevertheless, there exists a plethora of potential companions with whom you may foster a harmonious bond and from whom you could derive personal and emotional growth in the realm of love.

What is the significance of compatibility in interpersonal relationships?

When in the company of individuals with whom they are ill-suited, they experience a lack of satisfaction. Regrettably, we do not always exercise prudent judgment when selecting our partners. Subconsciously, individuals may find themselves attracted to others due to factors stemming from their childhood adaptations. The psychological barriers that we developed in our formative years played a pivotal role in facilitating our adjustment to the socio-cultural environment we grew up in. However, there is a growing realization that these barriers might impose certain limitations on our adult interpersonal connections.

In order to effectively adapt, we often seek companions who exhibit a comparable demeanor to that which was encountered within our familial environment. On an unconscious level, we often engage in regular exploration for individuals who do not align optimally with our requirements. For example, in the event that you frequently maintain a reserved demeanor and you are partnered with someone who is boisterous, you could potentially refrain from asserting yourself. Abandoning your partner's decisions and granting them sole authority in the relationship can potentially hinder your ability to assert yourself or achieve your desires.

Given the roles we assumed within our respective families, this particular pattern may initially evoke a sense of warmth and familiarity. However, with time, spouses
Oftentimes, individuals may harbor feelings of resentment and anger towards certain qualities in their partner that previously seemed highly appealing.

The initial allure we feel towards an individual eventually transforms into a sense of aversion when our connection with them is founded on disconcerting traits that harmonize effectively. An individual whom we initially favored for being "reliable" might subsequently be perceived as "uninteresting," whereas an individual we admired for being "charismatic" could soon be seen as "self-centered."

The quest for a suitable life partner ought to abstain from resembling a pursuit for our "lost fragment"; searching for an individual who "fulfills" us can impose limitations on our personal growth and potentially lead us to select partners based on misguided rationales. We ought to select those options that facilitate our personal development. Due to their heightened level of attentiveness and care, which exceeds what we are accustomed to or find reassuring, we may even become inclined to engage with individuals who initially elicit feelings of unease.

What is the most effective method for finding a compatible partner in a relationship?

Paradoxically, establishing compatibility within a relationship occasionally necessitates venturing beyond one's comfort zone. The paramount consideration in your selection is to opt for a partner with whom you genuinely enjoy your time. Do not excessively limit your choices by considering demographic factors such as age, profession, socioeconomic status, and so forth. Despite sustaining an injury, maintaining a receptive perspective is more advisable than yielding to the inclination to become more discerning or establish more intricate criteria for a compatible partner.

It is imperative to take into account the previous patterns of dating that did not yield favorable outcomes in the long term. What fundamental factors have negatively impacted your interpersonal connections? Are you inclined to exhibit a tendency towards excessively critical behavior towards others? Do you exert conscious intent in shaping the progression of the connection? Do you frequently extend the benefit of presumption to your partner? One can effectively discern the authentic self from the detrimental adaptations formed due to past distressing experiences through the identification of defense mechanisms and self-critical inner dialogues.

Do you hold the belief that compatibility in relationships is influenced by the principles of astrology or numerology?
In terms of any of these factors and their impact on compatibility in relationships, my understanding is somewhat limited. Nevertheless, I opine that their efficacy lies in their ability to inspire individuals to cultivate relationships or be receptive

to the pursuit of love. In contrast, individuals can employ any form of input to establish limitations on their own behavior or to harbor unfavorable perceptions of potential partners.

Irrespective of one's particular perspective, it is imperative to harbor unwavering belief in one's capacity for transformation and in one's own self. Irrespective of your inherent disposition (be it determined by genetics or astrology), you have the ability to alter certain aspects of yourself that you find undesirable or hindering in the development of close personal connections.

Is it indispensable to select a companion with whom you harmonize in every facet of existence? Alternatively, "Do certain circumstances deem compatibility with your romantic partner more pivotal than others?"

There is no singular individual on this planet with whom you will be entirely compatible. In the quest for relationship compatibility, one might endeavor to find an individual who demonstrates an inclination towards embracing novel experiences, being receptive to feedback, and striving for personal growth. One is inviting complications by seeking a solitary individual to meet all of their desires. Although having congruent beliefs can be advantageous, it is also typical for individuals in a relationship to possess disparate interests. It is imperative for couples to provide mutual encouragement for their joint interests and endeavors. Furthermore, they are required to demonstrate a willingness to engage in and actively explore each other's recreational interests. Do not confine your relationship or yourself within a restrictive framework. Make a constant effort to carry out acts of affection in a manner that would be deemed loving by an impartial observer. For a relationship to be harmonious, both individuals must possess a genuine concern for each other and consistently demonstrate admiration, regard, and assistance for one another's autonomy.

Dating a Police/Military

Maintaining an intimate relationship with an individual serving in the military or law enforcement presents distinctive and unparalleled challenges that diverge significantly from the difficulties encountered in relationships with civilian partners. It is not unexpected to observe certain females being drawn to careers in the armed forces and law enforcement. These individuals have devoted themselves to safeguarding the fundamental rights that are highly esteemed by societies, as well as upholding the principles that these societies hold dear. Many individuals are drawn to the military and police lifestyle due to a multitude of reasons.

There exist individuals who are drawn to the uniform in its own right, while others derive pleasure from the diversity that accompanies reassignments to novel and exhilarating geographic locations. While there are individuals who hold equivalent morals and values as the servicemen in question. For whichever personal motives one may have in pursuing a relationship with an individual serving in the military or police force, distinctive attributes distinguish armed forces and law enforcement personnel from the average civilian.

These individuals donning the attire of their respective professions consistently evoke profound emotions in their companions spanning numerous eras, regardless of their diverse origins. Be it the fashionable attire or the impeccably sculpted physique, the harmonious coordination and disciplined realm of their existence. Uniformed gentlemen possess a certain allure that appeals to women's sensibilities. Although. Their presence is inconsistent, as they appear intermittently and can remain absent for extended periods of time. It is perfectly logical to hold a favorable opinion of these uniformed individuals, whether they belong to the armed forces or law enforcement. For individuals engaged in a romantic rendezvous with a gentleman in military service, their boundless fortitude undoubtedly serves as a driving force.

If you appear to be enthralled by this self-assured young man who distinguishes himself from the masses with his polished footwear and an aura of heroism surrounding him. There are actions you ought to undertake in order to prompt him to approach you and initiate an interrogation. Allow me to provide you with some valuable insights into the process of initiating a romantic connection with a gentleman who is serving in either the army or the police force.

• Be considerate of their need for privacy. • Show regard for their personal space. • Honor their right to privacy.

One aspect of his role is to refrain from being outspoken and instead, assertively implement measures. It is possible that he possesses certain confidential matters he would prefer to retain solely within himself, thus electing not to disclose them to you.

• Align yourself with their actions.

The military personnel and law enforcement officers exhibit a propensity for discipline, thereby adhering to certain standards of order, such as punctuality and adherence to strict timetables. Now would be an opportune moment to establish organizational strategies, ensuring that impeccable order and cleanliness are maintained to convey your competence and ability to effectively handle the responsibilities at hand.

• Display adaptability.

If you possess a preference for frequent companionship with your romantic partner, be prepared to endure extended periods of solitude. The rationale behind this is that these individuals in military attire may be summoned for duty at any given moment. Therefore, it is necessary to adapt your demeanor and emotions accordingly. If that is not the case, it is possible that you may not be well-suited for pursuing a romantic relationship with an individual serving in the military or law enforcement.

• Place your trust in him. • Have faith in his abilities. • Rely on him for support. • Entrust him with your confidence. • Count on him to meet your expectations.

In the event of a sustained relationship with a member of the military or law enforcement, the preservation of romance can be ensured through the presence of authentic sincerity and unwavering trust. This is due to the fact that your time together will invariably be constrained. Therefore, it is imperative to acknowledge and place trust in the statements relayed by your partner within that brief duration.

• Avoid exhibiting excessive control.

It is important to bear in mind that individuals in service-oriented professions often possess a propensity for assuming leadership roles. Simultaneously, it is worth noting that many individuals in such professions diligently strive to satisfy their chosen significant others. If one desires to prolong the duration of the date, it is advisable to refrain from exerting excessive control over circumstances or making excessive demands. These service members were formerly subject to ceaseless strain, yet they also hold high regard for women who afford them some leniency.

- Engage in direct personal communication. • Convey information through individual interaction. • Establish direct interpersonal communication.

Effective communication plays a crucial role in fostering healthy relationships, particularly in the context of long-distance dating. It is imperative that these couples cultivate a robust foundation for their relationship in order to facilitate unimpeded communication in the event of relocations. In order to demonstrate your affection, it is recommended to convey your emotions through written expressions or verbal exchanges during conversation. This approach, which has been tried and verified over a significant period of time, serves as an effective means to communicate your heartfelt sentiments, indicating your deep regard for him. It would be beneficial for you to maintain a record of daily activities and thoughts, enabling you to subsequently organize and incorporate them while composing emails to your partner.

• Ensure that every moment is meaningful and of high quality. • Strive to make every occasion a valuable and enriching experience. • Commit to maximizing the quality of every interaction and engagement. • Make it a priority to cultivate substance and significance in each instance. • Dedicate yourself to ensuring that every moment is imbued with exceptional value.

When your service provider is present, possibly during a brief respite, ensure that you are in a positive emotional state and that your mindset is attuned to fostering romantic connections. While you are residing in that particular period, invest your time primarily in interlocking his hands with yours, exchanging affectionate gazes, and engaging in intimate conversations within a secluded and peaceful setting. Gently express your affection to him by whispering in his ear that you love him every time he departs. This will invigorate him and ensure he remains contemplative of your presence.

There are additional recommendations to be taken into account should you feel confident in managing them; in such case, you are prepared to proceed. Sustaining a genuine bond necessitates exertion, and acquiring a profound comprehension of the intricate dynamics of a military or police partner's life can lead to an exceptional and fulfilling relationship.

1. Yield Command

It is important to comprehend that individuals serving in the military and law enforcement possess limited influence over their personal lives and allocation of time. They lead altruistic existences, and there will come a moment when you will no longer, and indeed cannot, occupy the highest position of importance in your partner's life. This implies neither disregard nor lack of acknowledgment towards your worth or gratitude. It is simply inherent to the nature of the occupation. One must be prepared to assume a subservient role when responsibilities demand.

2. Do you also lead a military or police lifestyle?

When entering into a romantic relationship with an individual serving in the military or law enforcement, you will bid farewell to your previous existence and embark upon a unique and extraordinary journey. You will encounter military deployments and emotionally challenging separations, while the reunions upon returning home will resemble blissful second honeymoons. The allies of your partner will subsequently align with you. One will perpetually remain concerned about the inherent hazards associated with their occupation. The conventional way of living will not seamlessly integrate into your life without notice. Its mighty roar will profoundly transform your true essence.

3. Requesting Assistance

There may arise instances wherein feelings of sadness and frustration might be experienced. The experience of loneliness can potentially lead to a profound sense of depression that may overcome an individual. The occurrence of these emotional sentiments is unavoidable within a military relationship, and it is imperative to confront them directly. One optimal approach entails locating a support network. A variety of support groups and online communities have been specifically developed to cater to the needs of military spouses. Engaging in conversation with acquaintances and family members may also prove beneficial.

In order for long-distance relationships to thrive, it is imperative that both individuals demonstrate a shared commitment to resolving obstacles jointly. Gaining the knowledge of initiating a romantic relationship with a gentleman in uniform is a straightforward task, yet ensuring its longevity and stability proves to be quite formidable.

Display your jovial demeanor to him.

When preparing for your upcoming meeting with the individual, it is advisable to attire yourself in a slightly more formal manner compared to your previous encounters. Given that this event will take place during the evening hours and involves the consumption of beverages, you may opt to dress in a slightly more formal manner if you so desire. During a casual discourse, you may feel more at ease to disclose additional information about yourself while enjoying some refreshments. Inform him regarding your family, acquaintances, or professional affiliations. If he is interested in you, he will likely inquire about various matters. Maintain honesty and proceed with a deliberate pace during your conversation. This is not a romantic outing; you will be meeting a friend for a social gathering over drinks and nothing further. Keep in mind that your goal is not to make a strong impression on him at this juncture; rather, endeavor to communicate a few aspects of your personality that highlight your enjoyable qualities.

Now is the opportune moment to disclose your preference for engaging in mountain jogging or cycling to him. Presently is an opportune moment to disclose to him your fondness for NASCAR, bowling, and embarking on extensive road trips. Allow him to experience your lightheartedness. Allow him to witness a distinct facet of your personality, one that sets you apart from the multitude of other females vying for his attention incessantly. It is highly likely that you will express something to his liking as well. At this point, it is appropriate to redirect the conversation back towards him. When he expresses his passion for cross-country travel, initiate a discussion regarding the enjoyable destinations he has encountered throughout the nation. When he reminisces about a location that you have also been to, engage in conversation about all the enjoyable activities and experiences that occurred during your trip together. The crucial aspect lies in maintaining a consistent conversation revolving around enjoyable topics, pleasurable moments, thrilling escapades, and delightful encounters. As he commutes home this evening, the prominent idea lingering in his mind will be the extent to which she personifies a delightful woman.

There exists a significant distinction between a girl who enjoys having fun and a girl who actively seeks out fun experiences. He has encountered a considerable number of women who seek amusement, and you are likely a rejuvenating departure from that pattern in his current circumstances. It is important to maintain a consistently positive outlook on the experiences one encounters, as this reflects the individual as an individual with a light-hearted character, even during the most challenging circumstances. Due to a mechanical failure of your vehicle during the journey towards the Grand Canyon, you resorted to spending the night outdoors beneath the starry skies, ultimately finding great enjoyment in the experience. That appears to be significantly more captivating than listening to a narrative about how a punctured tire greatly disrupted a significant portion of your journey. You possess a plethora of commendable qualities, as well as a corresponding number of areas for improvement. There is unquestionably no fault in directing one's attention to the positive aspects; rather, it is an inherent facet of your being and a truly admirable characteristic. If you recollect a past occasion when you were engaged in operating a vehicle and enacted an action of such foolish nature that it presently elicits amusement, why not consider sharing that particular encounter with him. He would likely derive great pleasure from it. It demonstrates your capacity for vulnerability, while subtly indicating your ability to maintain a sense of self-deprecating humor. Please ensure you bear in mind that this encompasses more than just your personal interests. Many young women become excessively engrossed in this phase, preventing the guy from expressing himself. Include some information about yourself while allowing the individual to share their own experiences as well. You may not be aware of it currently, but you are unknowingly making a strong impression on him through qualities that are hidden from your perception. He is discerning that you possess qualities such as attentive listening, self-deprecating humor, and a measured, unhurried approach towards developing this relationship. By the conclusion of this meeting, it is imperative that it becomes evident to both parties involved that there is an underlying situation at hand. The subsequent logical progression entails the arrangement of a formal rendezvous. The occasion could take the form of a dinner, a movie, or alternatively, a romantic stroll on the beach, weather permitting. Kindly inform him of your availability this weekend and proceed to arrange a suitable venue for your inaugural formal outing together. If you recall from the preliminary , I advised against establishing the foundation of the relationship upon falsehoods at its inception. Could you perceive the potential distress that would arise from the necessity of perpetuating deceit? You are making considerable strides, and the foundation of this relationship is predicated upon thus far verifiable facts. Today, your likelihood of successfully pursuing the individual who embodies your aspirations has significantly improved. Start preparing for your significant rendezvous, and we shall proceed to discuss strategies for evading the pitfalls of being subjected to the "friend zone" in the subsequent section.

Six: Strategies for circumventing the ensnarement of the Friend Trap

Prior to embarking on the rendezvous with the individual who encapsulates your aspirations, it is imperative for you to comprehend the significant gravity of this forthcoming juncture. During the course of this rendezvous, you will engage in more profound conversations, and it is quite common for young women to feel compelled to make a favorable impression on their male counterparts regardless of the consequences. One of the major errors you could commit at this juncture is to appear excessively informal or familiar. He already possesses a considerable number of male acquaintances, and should you adopt behaviors akin to those of his companions, he shall extend the same treatment towards you as he does to them. The most straightforward avenue for you to potentially be ensnared in the friend trap is to consistently acquiesce to all of his statements. Upon his disclosure of his fondness for the Padres, an ardent admiration for the team ensues within you. Upon hearing his statement expressing his enjoyment of Duck Dynasty, you respond by affirming your fondness for the same television show. He expresses his fondness for Sundays, as they afford him the opportunity to recline on the sofa and indulge in viewing vintage films. In response, you kindly inform him that you partake in this very activity each Sunday as well.

This is the most straightforward path to inadvertently becoming stuck in the realm of platonic camaraderie. By expressing your affinity for all his interests, you diminish the distinctiveness that initially captivated him towards you. By now, it can be safely assumed that his intentions towards you extend beyond mere friendship. Do not inadvertently convey misleading cues to him by displaying interest in subjects that genuinely hold no appeal to you. He might be in search of a female companion who possesses an affinity for engaging in regular excursions to the seaside for the purpose of indulging in recreational fishing activities. If you were to disclose your affinity for angling to him, you must brace yourself for numerous extended weekends permeated with the odor of entrails belonging to aquatic creatures. If you possess no affinity for fishing, refrain from falsely claiming an interest in order to sustain the growth of this relationship.

In addition to the ongoing necessity of maintaining this façade for an extended duration, it is also inequitable towards the gentleman in question. He could potentially be in a similar predicament as yourself, and given the extent of being deceived over the course of numerous years, he could be genuinely delighted to have discovered a young woman who shares a deep affection for his passions. How do you anticipate his reaction when he becomes aware that you were misleading him? When one exhibits agreement with all his statements and affection for everything he holds dear, they inherently fit into the classification of a friend. You are merely an acquaintance who enjoys partaking in alcoholic beverages together, and perhaps a more undesirable scenario is that of a friend who engages in a casual sexual relationship. Engaging in a casual sexual relationship not only constitutes a significant form of self-disregard, but also has the potential to adversely influence one's standing within the local community by perpetuating a perception of readily satisfying male desires. A man who genuinely values and appreciates you will never seek to exploit you based solely on your physical appearance. True gentlemen recognize and admire your worth beyond superficial qualities, understanding that a fulfilling relationship is built on deeper connection and mutual respect. Once you enter a purely platonic friendship with such an individual, the opportunity for a genuine romantic involvement becomes increasingly unlikely.

Today, you may experience some degree of apprehension as you embark on your inaugural romantic rendezvous. This does not imply that you must succumb and discard all the diligent efforts that have brought you to this juncture. Employ methods to calm yourself and acknowledge that your objective is no longer focused on capturing his affection. He is intending to engage in a social outing with you; therefore, cease your attempts to solicit his admiration. It is imperative that you display vulnerability and reveal your true self to him, allowing him to envision the potential for a meaningful and romantic connection between the two of you. Display self-assurance, exhibit courtesy, and above all else, derive enjoyment from the experience. One of the ways you can impress him now is by impressing his friends. Shall we proceed to the next ?

27. Engage in romantic encounters with individuals who understand and appreciate you.

When embarking on the search for your life partner, it may be necessary to fully immerse yourself in several romantic involvements. If one is fortunate, they may encounter their soul mate upon experiencing love for the first time, or it may require multiple subsequent attempts to do so.

It is imperative to associate oneself with individuals who possess a deep understanding of one's thought processes and perspectives. In fact, provided that both parties possess a mutual comprehension of their respective goals and aspirations, there exists no necessity to complete each other's sentences.

28. Engage in a physical altercation.

One's propensity to handle conflicts reveals their level of compatibility. Thus, it is essential to attentively observe your initial combat performance and assess your progress.

29. Be amiable

Ensure that you consistently maintain an attitude of politeness, openness, and a warm smile. By doing so, you will increase the likelihood of capturing someone's attention and initiating a conversation.

30. Confront a difficult predicament collaboratively

One can determine whether an individual is truly their soulmate by subjecting them to a series of rigorous assessments.

31. Don\\\'t hide your emotions.

Frequently, despite being aware of their incorrectness, individuals commonly choose to remain in detrimental relationships. Trust your instincts. Do not disregard the emotion if it is present.

32. Give it time

Please endeavor to exercise patience and refrain from becoming excessively agitated, as the process of finding the suitable individual may require a significant amount of time.

33. Please make a record of past communications.

Previous romantic partnerships have imparted crucial wisdom provided that one assimilates the insights gleaned from those experiences. And utilize them for the purpose of educating your new additions.

34. Enjoy being single.

Please bear in mind that you must not allow your pursuit of a soulmate to dominate your existence. Endeavor to find solace in the experience of being unattached.

35. Remain vigilant and exercise patience until satisfaction is assured prior to making a decision.

In matters of love, it is advisable to engage in compromise, but it is not necessary to excessively exert yourself in order to maintain your partner's happiness. Concession is an inherent aspect of love, yet it must be a reciprocal effort.

If one finds themselves developing romantic feelings for another person, yet lacks substantial enthusiasm or realizes they are exerting excessive efforts to sustain the relationship, it would be advisable to disengage and refrain from dwelling on it further. Despite the appearance of self-interest, genuine love should exhibit simplicity. Should one ever discover that their happiness is compromised within a relationship, one ought to respectfully disengage and conscientiously continue seeking a compatible partner.

Why persist in a suboptimal partnership when the possibility of experiencing profound joy awaits upon discovering a compatible soulmate? There exists an ideal life partner who is also actively seeking a compatible match like yourself.

36. Acquire a profound comprehension of the essence and significance of a soulmate.

Exhibit genuine sincerity when delineating the concept of a soulmate. They do not possess the exceptional qualities to comprehend and fulfill your every need. Occasionally errors are made, however, it is acceptable. Exercise patience and refrain from hastily terminating a relationship solely based on occasional imperfections.

Are you currently in search of your life partner? If one adheres to these instructions while traversing the path of love, they shall undoubtedly acquire the key to expediting the discovery of their soul mate beyond their expectations.

7. Do not accept mediocrity.

Avoid making the error of compromising for less solely for the sake of expediting the search for a compatible life partner.

Take into account the individual and the relationship you wish to establish.

Although it is permissible for you to pursue romantic relationships with others during this period, it is essential to maintain honesty with them regarding your intentions and have the discernment to withdraw gracefully if they do not align with your long-term desires.

8. Be cheerful.

While anticipating the arrival of your destined life partner, it is advisable to derive pleasure from the present moments of existence. If you are discontent, others will be unable to bring about your happiness.

Take into account all the aspects of your life for which you feel gratitude and the experiences that have bestowed abundant happiness upon you. Additionally, you can commence engaging in a greater number of activities that bring you joy. Don\\\'t starve yourself.

9. Preexisting notions can have adverse effects on business operations.
It is possible that you had anticipated discovering your true love by this point, yet such a desire remains unfulfilled. This might cause you to perceive yourself as a spinster or as inadequate, but such thinking presents a potentially perilous situation.

It might be more advantageous to employ positive affirmations of love in order to entice compatible partners, instead of harboring negative thoughts.

10. be flexible and adaptable.
In order to discover your genuine affection and encounter the companionship of a kindred spirit, you

must demonstrate a willingness to acclimate to novel circumstances and possess a flexible demeanor. Stated differently, it will be necessary for you to allocate space in your life for a potential companion and make the necessary arrangements for a complete transformation of your life.

11. Do not wager against the inevitable.
It is possible that you hold the belief that you will encounter your life partner in the near future, although the exact timing remains uncertain. Retain your assurance that it will come to fruition. In the event that one experiences uncertainty or develops a belief that their soulmate is unattainable, it is plausible that feelings of despair may ensue.

12. Sever ties with prior associations.

If you continue to harbor emotions for a former partner or engage in periodic encounters with an ex, it is advisable to cease such behavior. It is advisable to refrain from contemplating past romantic partners, whenever possible. It is undesirable to hold feelings of love for your soulmate while simultaneously being preoccupied with thoughts of other individuals. This constitutes an act of injustice towards any of you.

13. Remain calm and approach everything with composure.

All occurrences in your existence will inevitably leave a discernible influence on your being. You ought to possess the capability to handle any circumstances that may arise. Remain receptive and bear in mind that the person destined to be your soulmate might make their appearance when you are least anticipating it.

In the event that further aid is desired, it is recommended to seek the guidance of a therapist for the purpose of addressing trauma or other difficulties.

14. Maintain honesty with oneself

It is imperative to maintain truthfulness with oneself as one embarks on the journey of attracting their soulmate. It is imperative that you exhibit honesty regarding your expectations and desired characteristics for your life partner. This might not prove advantageous if you hold impractical fairy tale ideas.

15. Improve yourself

In the interim of awaiting your compatible life partner, it is advisable to engage in personal development. Maybe you aspire to acquire swimming proficiency or would like to refine your dart throwing expertise.

Now is the perfect occasion to accomplish it. Additionally, it can furnish you with a conversational topic following your encounter with the person destined to be your partner.

16. Maintain a positive outlook regarding the future.
Being optimistic about the future confers numerous benefits. Despite the uncertainty of what lies ahead, one can still anticipate the future with optimism. In spite of adversities, maintaining a positive mindset may exert a comparatively lesser detrimental impact on one's mental well-being as compared to succumbing to despair.

17. Try something novel.
If you have diligently sought a compatible life partner for an extensive duration without encountering the ideal

match, it is opportune to explore novel alternatives.

You may consider exploring online dating applications or engaging in social gatherings outside traditional venues, such as bars or clubs. If deemed essential, you have the option to solicit guidance from acquaintances.

18. Maintain your belief that it will come to fruition for you.

Certain individuals hold the belief that every person has a perfect counterpart, and as such, it is imperative to consistently maintain the conviction that one can indeed discover their ideal life partner. This exemplifies the importance of displaying patience and allowing individuals to approach you in due time.

Enduring the period of waiting may prove to be challenging, yet the anticipated outcome is highly likely to justify the effort.

19. Imagine your soulmate

While you await, you have the opportunity to envision the potential appearance of your partner. Do you anticipate that they will have a darker complexion? Alternatively, he or she might possess a tall and lean physique.

When it comes to encountering your prospective life partner, employing the law of attraction in this endeavor can prove to be highly effective, as it may increase the likelihood of encountering them in person, bearing resemblance to the image you have visualized. One cannot ascertain the outcome without making an attempt.

20. Please engage in a written discussion regarding the matter.

Under specific circumstances, documenting your ideas on strategies to allure your true life partner can prove advantageous. Jotting down your thoughts on paper can be instrumental in achieving mental clarity and cultivating a positive mindset. Engaging in the practice of journaling can also provide effective assistance in alleviating stress.

21. Allocate space for them within the confines of your existence.

Does there exist sufficient space for a companion? If you have not already done so, it is advisable for you to establish a designated area for them. You may have the need to procure a larger bed or reassess the manner in which you have furnished the room.

Take into consideration the alterations you would anticipate from another individual in order to facilitate your determination regarding the necessary modifications.

22. Make arrangements for your partner
While you are endeavoring to ready your life for a companion, it is imperative to additionally equip yourself for the same. Are you ready to receive affection and establish a long-lasting connection with another individual?
Give thoughtful consideration to this matter, ensuring that you are fully prepared to collaborate with your prospective soulmate.

23. Keep going.
When one dedicates a substantial duration towards acquiring the knowledge of appealing to their soulmate, it should not be expected that the culmination of this pursuit will occur instantaneously. Do not despair; instead, remain steadfast in the knowledge that circumstances will align in due course.
There is no necessity to rush into anything.

24. Do not delay in indulging in leisure activities.

Please be mindful that there is no need for you to delay commencing the pursuit of a fulfilling existence. Although you may not have discovered your ultimate source of happiness, it does not preclude you from experiencing enjoyment and contentment in your life.

Engage in pastimes that bring you joy and indulge in small moments of self-reward.

SEX N DATING

Regardless of your level of experience in the dating world, be it as a newcomer, an expert, or someone reentering after a considerable hiatus, the ensuing inquiries pertaining to dating protocols deserve consideration: How expeditiously should one lean in upon initiating a first kiss? Is it premature to engage in intimate physical contact? In conclusion, may I inquire as to when it is deemed suitable to partake in sexual intercourse?

"I have not had the opportunity to observe any formula," expressed Andrew Reyes, a 29-year-old resident of Baltimore, Maryland. It is contingent upon the speed at which things progress.

According to the research conducted by Joan Allen, a renowned authority in the field of relationships, it has been revealed that individuals belonging to the baby boomer generation are significantly more inclined to delay engaging in sexual activities compared to their younger counterparts.

According to Allen, the author of Celebrating Single and Getting Love Right: From Stalemate to Soulmate, older individuals who have personally observed the sexual revolution tend to acknowledge the existence of emotional repercussions associated with participating in a sexual relationship.

Based on the individuals Allen has encountered, it can be observed that there exists a notable disparity in the dating norms followed by individuals belonging to different age brackets, namely baby boomers and young adults in their 20s.

She recollects a conversation she had with a young gentleman in his early to mid-twenties, who expressed his intention to seek another partner if he did not engage in sexual activity during the initial encounters.

Although there isn't a universally applicable solution for establishing sexual dating guidelines, professionals recommend devising a set of judicious dating rules prior to the significant encounter.

Why is it important to patiently await the issuance of dating guidelines?

Allen and other authorities in the field recommend exercising prudence when it pertains to adhering to guidelines for sexual relationships.

Allen suggests exercising patience and waiting for as long as feasibly possible.

The rationale behind these dating regulations may seem apparent, yet numerous individuals tend to overlook them amidst intense emotions. You may come to realize that you do not have a favorable opinion of the individual.

Concurring with other specialists, it is widely acknowledged that engaging in sexual activity prematurely can entail potential risks.

Would you be interested in engaging in a dance with me? According to Susanne Alexander, a renowned relationship coach and acclaimed author, the task of objectively evaluating each other's character traits becomes significantly more challenging.

Subsequently, certain couples choose to commence matrimonial relations, only to subsequently become aware that they have overlooked significant facets of one another.

She recalls conversing with a young gentleman, approximately in his early to mid-twenties, who expressed that in the event he did not engage in sexual activity within the first or second evening, he would seek other prospects.

Although there is no universally applicable solution for establishing sexual dating protocols, professionals recommend formulating a set of judicious guidelines prior to the anticipated encounter.

Why is it Necessary to Await Dating Guidelines?

Allen and other reputable authorities in the field strongly advocate exercising prudence with regards to rules surrounding sexual relationships in a general context.

Allen suggests waiting for as long as one feasibly can.

In the context of romantic relationships, it is advisable to engage in verbal communication before taking any concrete actions.
Although not all dating experiences involving sexual activity culminate in marriage or a committed partnership, it is important for couples to engage in a conversation regarding the future trajectory of their relationship and the potential effects that engaging in sexual activity may have, prior to engaging in such activities.

A preliminary discourse is necessary. A woman may hold the belief that engaging in sexual activity signifies a mutual commitment, while a man may not subscribe to the same perspective."

Primarily, engage in introspection.

According to experts, engaging in open and honest conversations about sexual matters, both with oneself and with one's partner, holds equal significance.

Prior to entering into a romantic relationship, it is essential for both women and men to have a clear understanding of their personal limits and boundaries. However, as confirmed by Cheryl McClary, PhD, JD, a distinguished professor specializing in women's health at the University of North Carolina-Asheville, it is unfortunately common for the majority of individuals to lack this understanding.

When McClary discusses boundaries, she goes beyond mere reference to the physical limitations inherent in sexual contexts. In addition, she is engaging in a discourse regarding the establishment of emotional boundaries.

In the process of determining whether or not to engage in sexual activity, emotional well-being is of paramount importance.
If prioritizing a dedicated partnership holds significance for you, it is advisable to ponder introspectively, 'What measures must I undertake to maintain my emotional well-being?' McClary frequently imparts counsel to female individuals.

McClary adopts a distinct perspective on dating guidelines when engaging with a male demographic. She advises ensuring that your intellect, emotions, and physical desires are harmonized, aligning them in a linear fashion before engaging in sexual activity.

According to McClary, it is imperative for individuals engaging in dating to allocate a significant amount of time towards introspectively deliberating on their personal dating guidelines, in a manner comparably meticulous to that of preparing oneself aesthetically before a consequential rendezvous. Furthermore, she maintains the belief that engaging in a discussion, akin to the process of grooming oneself, should occur prior to the significant rendezvous.

McClary suggests contemplating one's sexual boundaries prior to consuming any alcoholic beverages.

Practical Dating Advice

Professionals recommend that after you have established your desired objectives for a date, it is essential to incorporate the act of disclosing this information to your partner as a standard practice within your dating strategies.

It is your obligation to communicate to your partner that your intent is solely to engage in a sexual encounter, if you seek a transient relationship. Although this information may not be well-received by a romantic partner, it has the potential to mitigate future disillusionments.

The objective of engaging in a candid dialogue concerning sexually transmitted diseases is equivalent to that of talking about STDs.\\\"It is imperative to engage in conversations regarding the potential perils of STDs and adopt preventive measures,\\\" she strongly advises, recommending the use of condoms even within established partnerships.

McClary posits that demonstrating apprehension towards sexually transmitted diseases and unintended pregnancies can assist individuals in setting clear and defined limits within their intimate relationships. If one is contemplating an escalation in their sexual endeavors, a prudent level of apprehension might prompt hesitance, particularly if one is unready to employ the appropriate safeguards. Furthermore, a lack of proper preparation for these practical aspects of sexual activity can suggest a general absence of preparedness for engaging in such behavior.

Numerous romantic couples opt to breach their initial emotional, physical, or both boundaries during the course of their courtship, engaging in a sexual relationship. Such an intimate connection may serve as a pathway to a consensual and committed union, contingent upon both individuals adhering to shared principles and protocols of dating.

From my understanding, individuals of varying genders tend to possess divergent viewpoints when it comes to relationships. "But it has been found that they often desire the same outcome," Allen asserts.

Effective Communication Strategies: Establishing Effective Communication with Your Partner

A soulmate is an individual who fills the missing piece in one's heart. They serve as your closest companion, your chosen companion during meals, the individual whom you approach for guidance, and the individual whom you cannot fathom a life without. Maintaining a robust and thriving relationship necessitates the establishment of effective communication channels with a kindred spirit. There are multiple conduits for establishing communication with your Soul We posit that by following these prescribed procedures, you will be able to establish a robust framework for fostering effective communication with your romantic partner.

Practice Emotional Intimacy

Prior to delving into the procedural aspects, we wish to underscore a crucial aspect. Soulmates cannot exist in isolation. Consequently, it will be necessary for you to effectively articulate your emotions and communicate your personal encounters. If one possesses the ability to express emotions with their Soul Companion, they shall thereby enhance their proficiency in communicating with them. It is now appropriate to initiate the progression towards establishing emotional intimacy.

Emotional intimacy refers to the capacity to freely express one's emotions and share personal experiences with one's Soulmate. Although it may not always be feasible to openly communicate your emotions with your partner, you have the ability to exchange your experiences with them. Think about it. In the absence of your partner, who will be there to provide you with the necessary support during challenging circumstances?

There exist three methodologies by which one may convey their emotions.

By telling

When expressing your emotions, you are communicating to your Soulmate regarding your current feelings, experiences, and thoughts. This serves as an excellent means of expressing your emotional state to your partner.

By showing

When one displays their emotions to their Soulmate, they communicate their innermost feelings and convey their current state of being. This constitutes a significant aspect of the emotional intimacy procedure. Negative emotions are not always necessary. Indeed, it can also have positive implications.

By doing

During joint activities, it is important to communicate your emotions to your significant other. This approach can also prove to be highly effective in facilitating communication. It can be as uncomplicated as collaborating in the operation of a dishwasher. Alternatively, you may choose to undertake collaborative efforts towards effecting changes. The greater amount of practice you engage in when it comes to articulating your emotions, the more at ease you will grow in terms of opening up about your experiences. Once an individual gains the capacity to articulate their emotions and convey their personal encounters, they will attain the ability to engage in more profound levels of communication with their significant other. In order to effectively cultivate emotional intimacy, it is imperative that individuals consistently communicate their thoughts, emotions, and personal experiences. Try to be consistent.

Make sure you are adequately prepared to engage in a substantive conversation with your life partner. Engaging in dialogue requires active participation from both parties involved.

Have you ever experienced the sensation of being uniquely attuned to your Soul Companion, as if no other individual on this planet comprehends them in the same profound manner as you do? It is not an infrequent sentiment—indeed, locating a remarkable conversationalist can prove to be quite challenging. However, it has been discovered that a lack of engaging discourse with an individual does not render them incompatible with you. It is possible that you simply need to ascertain the optimal method of communication. The utmost crucial aspect to bear in mind regarding conversations is that a fruitful discourse cannot be achieved in the absence of attentive engagement. And one's ability to pay attention is impeded when one lacks interest in the discourse initiated by their Soulmate. Your counterpart is incapable of understanding your thoughts, nor can they intrude upon your internal dialogue. If it were within their capacity, they would certainly do so. They possess the ability to discern whether you are diverting your attention, or engaging in deep contemplation. The majority of individuals tend to selectively attend to certain aspects of their Soulmate's statements, failing to fully grasp and appreciate the entirety of their communication. Indeed, they may even lack awareness of the statements uttered by their Soulmate. Thus, endeavor to attain a state of calmness and release any anxieties or preoccupations that may burden you. Allow your significant other to articulate their thoughts, and afford yourself the opportunity to attentively receive their words.

Effective communication necessitates the comprehension of one's partner's perspective. Having the attribute of being a "attentive listener" does not imply passively allowing your significant other to speak without any interruption. It implies granting them the opportunity to express their thoughts or ideas verbally. Perhaps you may wish to interject periodically, and that is perfectly acceptable. However, it is important to allow your Soulmate to communicate without any disruptions. There is no obligation for you to concur with their viewpoints, or to develop a fondness for them. It suffices that you comprehend their perspective. Just listen. If you possess any inquiry, kindly pose it. If not, allow your significant other to speak. If you require an interruption of their conversation, in order to carefully ponder the content of their speech, execute such action. When your significant other endeavors to engage in conversation, kindly respond. If they attempt to engage in conversation with you, prohibit them from doing so. Upon receiving their input, you may proceed to engage in dialogue with them. It is permissible to engage in further conversations with them at a later time.

Do not hesitate to foster a sense of closeness in your communication with your Soulmate.

There is no necessity for you to proceed at a leisurely and gentle pace. You are free to fully embrace your sensuality and personal expression, while also extending an invitation for your Soulmate to do the same. It should be noted that the outcome of interpersonal communication directly influences the dynamics of a relationship, particularly since a relationship encompasses various facets of emotional bonding. One can exhibit qualities of sensuality and sensitivity without displaying attributes of sexual dominance. One can exhibit gentleness and kindness, as well as a playful demeanor. One does not necessarily need to maintain physical proximity with their Soulmate for the purpose of engaging in sexual activities, and displaying excessive gentleness and thoughtfulness is not a prerequisite for expressing tenderness. You may also exhibit assertiveness and high standards, but those attributes are acceptable as well. Indeed, you have the freedom to exhibit as much distinction from one another as you desire, and that is the fundamental objective. Individuals have the capacity to exhibit uniqueness, while simultaneously forming emotional connections. One can maintain individuality without experiencing a sense of disconnection.

I am unaware of any established precedent governing the appropriate timing for broaching the subject of one's romantic involvement. In my opinion, the outcome hinges upon various factors such as one's circumstances, emotional well-being, previous encounters, and the level of affinity experienced with one's Soulmate. I recall an anecdote concerning an acquaintance of mine who, having never engaged in romantic relationships previously, encountered an individual through online means. Both of them had been endeavoring to initiate a romantic connection for an extended period of time, yet neither of them succeeded in suppressing their emotions. Ultimately, they agreed upon a specific day and time. Despite feeling apprehensive, she remained confident in her ability to express her emotions upon their long-awaited encounter. They embarked on an initial rendezvous, which transpired favorably. The gentleman extended an invitation for a subsequent outing, and she acquiesced. Unbeknownst to her, they swiftly entered into a romantic partnership, culminating in the recent addition of their infant offspring.

From my perspective, a relationship can be likened to a blossoming flower. One establishes the relationship by sowing the seeds and nurturing its growth. In order to cultivate a thriving relationship, it is essential to nurture it. It is imperative that you allocate time for the nourishment, maintenance, and cultivation of this matter.

It is advisable to commence conversations regarding your relationship at a time when you feel at ease with the subject matter.

FOUR
Cultivate hearing God now!

This holds significant importance within the context of this book, and it is crucial to approach it with sincerity as the possibility of encountering the ideal partner may manifest unexpectedly, possibly even through unconventional channels. Do not individuals, possessing their inherent humanity, universally yearn for the solace and deliverance of a supreme entity during moments of distress? The deity that I am referring to in this context is the omniscient divine being who brought forth your existence and the individual whom you long for. He possesses a magnitude surpassing that of the world, yet He dwells within us and possesses the ability to transform anyone.

As an individual adhering to the Christian faith, I contemplate the potential trajectory my life may have taken had I not embraced Christ at an early stage. He is identified as Jesus Christ and He wishes to establish a connection with anyone who is open to extending an invitation to Him. Your current state is a reflection of His previous experiences with you, and there is no novelty in the aspects of your life that He is aware of. In fact, His understanding of you surpasses your own self-awareness. He desires to guide you through the process of selecting a lifelong companion. It is essential to acknowledge that marriage cannot prosper without His presence, thus it is advisable to embark on the marital journey in His company.

Prior to the arrival of your ideal partner, it is crucial that you cultivate a profound sense of divine connection and maintain a consistent and deep-seated spiritual relationship. Prior to entering into marriage, it is of utmost importance for you to possess the ability to perceive God's guidance on various other aspects. Certain individuals commit marital mistakes due to mistakenly attributing their personal thoughts, desires, and idealized notions of a spouse to divine guidance.

How can one distinguish between the voice of God and their own internal thoughts, particularly for individuals who already maintain a personal connection with the divine?

The notion that you reside in the preceding time frame of God provides the guarantee that He possesses knowledge of your forthcoming circumstances and the suitable individual destined for you, thereby rendering it impermissible to disregard the influence of God in this matter.

Upon receiving an invitation from the individual who caused me considerable emotional distress, I sought divine guidance through prayer. It was during this spiritual communion that I discerned God's instruction to exhibit forbearance and await with patience.

This individual appeared appealing; however, divine guidance did not reveal their suitability for me, but instead advised me to exercise patience. From a theological standpoint, he was a divine creation, thus prompting the question as to why the delay? I desired the presence of a gentleman in my life expeditiously, as I wished not to endure solitude for even a single day. I sought an individual who would consistently provide assurance, validation, and be incessantly attentive; one who would consistently express my beauty and profess their inability to exist without my companionship. Therefore, I proceeded without the divine consent. I had come to deeply lament the decision I had made.

Following the emotional turmoil, I sought solace in the divine presence, expressing remorse and declaring my willingness to patiently await divine guidance and fulfill divine wishes. In a clear-headed condition and following a period of reconnecting with my faith, I received a divine message. The voice of God conveyed to me, imparting the following words, "Devote the next six months solely to Me, abstaining from any romantic involvement with others. By the end of this six-month period, I shall bring forth your future spouse." Initially, I harbored doubts regarding my ability to adhere to this guidance, but I placed my trust in the divine and thus commenced my journey towards healing and restoration.

I terminated all romantic relationships, declined to engage in dating. Despite the fact that I maintained connections with friends who remained invested in me. It proved to be a challenging experience, as I lacked any form of social support, such as personal phone calls, regular check-ins, and uplifting text messages that could brighten my day. That was the first occasion in quite a while, during which I found myself not lacking potential admirers. However, I strongly felt the necessity to seek solace in solitude, in order to introspect and cultivate self-acceptance.

Furthermore, during my spiritual connection with the divine, I received a message from God which indicated that my husband was not yet in a stable financial position. However, I expressed my readiness to God, citing my own financial stability as evidence that this would not pose a significant hindrance.

After the conclusion of a six-month period, I finally encountered the individual who I believed to be my ideal partner. Regrettably, it became evident that he did not possess significant financial stability. He served as a pastor in a church where he was not remunerated but received a monthly stipend of 10,000 naira, which he solely allocated for transportation expenses. He faced significant challenges, yet he possessed a discerning mindset and displayed a diligent work ethic. Given the divine guidance I received, I was able to provide him with financial assistance, enabling him to pursue theological education and enhance his attire.

Presently, the situation has undergone a significant transformation. We are currently in a state of contented matrimony, blessed with a familial unit consisting of three offspring, comprising two males and a female. Over the past span of six years, he has dutifully assumed the role of my caretaker, demonstrating unwavering dedication and exhibiting no signs of weariness or grievances, particularly since I resigned from my professional endeavors subsequent to our nuptials.

The guidance bestowed upon you by divine providence prior to embarking on matrimony serves as your steadfast weapon to confront adversities that may emerge. Marriage was ordained by the divine; the presence of a higher power is indispensable for the success of any union. When you acquire proficiency in interpreting and perceiving divine guidance pertaining to various aspects, upon the advent of the appropriate moment for matrimony, you shall not be prone to misinterpretation.

For individuals who do not adhere to the Christian faith, the initial step towards establishing a connection with the divine is to commit oneself to Jesus Christ. Prior to pursuing anything further, a prerequisite is establishing a solid foundation in the form of a relationship.

CAUTION: It is imperative not to assume that you can postpone the acquisition of the ability to listen to the divine until the prospect of marriage draws near, for this may prove to be an untimely endeavor. Furthermore, it is crucial to note that it is not within God's purview to select your life partner; rather, this responsibility falls squarely upon your shoulders. However, it is of utmost importance to prioritize your relationship with God when deliberating upon the prospect of matrimony. It has been communicated by certain women that they have received divine revelations stating, "The individual who enters donning a green neckwear is the chosen one." In the event that three individuals enter while dressed in varying hues of green, it would result in a rather peculiar situation, reminiscent of a pickle (deliberate wordplay intended). Ultimately, you are still faced with the need to make a decision. What God does is present the possibilities for consideration, yet He abstains from making the ultimate decision on your behalf.

After a fortuitous encounter arranged by divine intervention, I found myself with two suitors vying for my hand in marriage. One of these suitors possessed significant financial wealth, while the other was a globetrotting explorer. In fact, the latter even took the initiative of approaching my grandmother to declare his intentions. However, I regretfully declined their proposals. I made the decision to collaborate and accompany the individual whom God had shared some information with me about. One can never make a mistake by faithfully heeding the word of God. Despite encountering obstacles, there will perpetually be a means of overcoming them, as divine support is assisting you.

Once you attain the ability to perceive the presence of God, you will gain insight into His essence and derive profound experiences. In the institution of matrimony, it is imperative to prioritize listening to divine guidance over the task of nurturing one's offspring, wouldn't you agree? Each child is unique; no two children will follow identical paths.

Certain matters may arise that can only be resolved through divine guidance. In my marital relationship, I frequently find myself guiding my husband away from certain actions or decisions. It is worth noting that more often than not, he is able to recognize the value in heeding my advice as it assists him in avoiding unnecessary complications or difficulties. As a spouse, it is essential to possess the capacity to perceive both in the material and immaterial realms. This discernment is unattainable without the ability to actively listen to the divine.

3
Systematic guidelines for effectively engaging with unfamiliar individuals

There are numerous approaches to encountering unfamiliar individuals. Initiate a conversation with a select group of individuals whom you encounter on a regular basis, such as the commuters on your daily bus route, the patrons at your local gym or park, or the recurring checkout operators at your preferred grocery store. (Please ensure that you take the necessary precautions to ensure your safety when encountering unfamiliar individuals.)

Being in the company of others - for example, convening at a publicly accessible location - can serve as an effective approach.

Alternative ways to express the same idea in formal tone: 1. Various options include participating in a sports team, joining a club or society related to a specific interest, or engaging in volunteer work. 2. Diverse possibilities entail becoming involved in a athletic collective, affiliating with an organization or association centered around a specific passion, or dedicating time to charitable endeavors. 3. Various avenues consist of joining a sports team, becoming a member of a club or association dedicated to a specific hobby, or contributing to community service initiatives. Contact your local council to acquire information regarding community gatherings or initiatives, or alternatively, pay a visit to your nearby civic institution or library - there is consistently a plethora of activities unfolding within your locality.

Not every approach will yield the same results for everyone, therefore, endeavor to explore several distinctive methodologies to ascertain which ones are effective for your specific circumstances. If your initial endeavor is unsuccessful, consider pursuing an alternative option. The booklet authored by Past Blue's Connections contains a few noteworthy insights tailored towards the older demographic.

The social organization has the capacity to distribute your time, experiences, and narratives among individuals, and vice versa, take heed of their contributions. Consistently, you will establish a circle of individuals in your existence who hold genuine concern for your well-being, reciprocated by your own sentiments towards them. Both your cerebral functions and physical well-being will experience advantageous outcomes.

Networking fosters societal progress
Interpersonal connections exert a significant impact on one's overall welfare, while simultaneously extending one's reach to a broader societal sphere.

People who spend more time together form happy and beneficial networks.

Remember Self-Love
Love constitutes a formidable inclination, with a propensity to heal. Although love cannot remedy all, nor prevent the development of mental health disorders, it promotes optimal well-being in both physical and emotional aspects.

The study demonstrates that cultivating affectionate and resilient relationships, in addition to receiving considerable social support from family and friends, play a vital role in enhancing mental well-being.

In the event that you possess a companion or confidant and both of you encounter challenges related to mental well-being, find solace in the fact that you provide mutual support to each other. Discover innovative approaches to pursue treatment, engage in therapy, actively listen and express emotions, and effectively resolve conflicts, enabling you to maintain a harmonious coexistence, despite the presence of maladaptive behaviors.

Making a definitive decision

Monetary currency might serve as a means to sustain a prosperous lifestyle. Furthermore, the ability to promptly pursue such choices and maintaining a discerning outlook on your problem-solving skills could effectively alleviate unnecessary time consumption and inconvenience.

Thankfully, each individual possesses the capacity to undertake the necessary steps to develop into more effective leaders. If you aspire to enhance your abilities as a leader, incorporate these nine daily habits into your lifestyle.

1 Observe Your Overconfidence
A lady making decisions within a group.
Empathetic Eye Foundation/Getty Images

Presumptuousness unquestionably leads to erroneous judgment. Various studies consistently demonstrate that individuals tend to inaccurately evaluate both their performance and the accuracy of their knowledge.

Perhaps you have a high level of confidence, approximately 90%, in your knowledge of the location of the workplace you are intending to visit. Alternatively, it is possible that you have a strong 80% conviction in your ability to convince your manager to grant you a promotion. If one becomes excessively arrogant or haughty regarding such matters, it is likely that their plans or preparations will result in unfavorable outcomes.

It is of utmost importance to carefully assess your level of certainty regarding the effective utilization of time. The overwhelming majority tends to underestimate the extent of their potential accomplishments within a given time frame. Do you anticipate that it will only require one hour of your time to finalize that report? Do you expect that you will be able to promptly settle your online financial obligations? You appear to be making unwarranted assumptions in your predictions.

Devote regular intervals to assess the likelihood of achieving success. Subsequently, subsequently, during the final hours, evaluate your assessments. Is it accurate to say that you were as precise as you anticipated?

Distinguished leaders identify areas in their lives where arrogance may pose a concern. Subsequently, they alter their rationale and adjust their conduct accordingly.

Identify and differentiate the risks you undertake.

Commonality breeds solace. Furthermore, it is highly probable that you may make several unfavorable choices due to the fact that you have become accustomed to your tendencies and do not fully contemplate the danger you are in or the harm you are causing.

As an example, one could engage in the act of driving at an accelerated pace while consistently commuting to their workplace. Upon each occasion that you arrive without incurring a speeding infraction, you gradually develop a greater level of comfort with driving at higher speeds. In any event, your well-being is being jeopardized and you are assuming a substantial risk.

Alternatively, it is plausible that you consistently opt for inexpensive meals during your lunchtime. As you display no immediate signs of illness, it is likely that you perceive it to be inconsequential. Nevertheless, in the long run, you may potentially experience weight gain or encounter other medical complications as a consequence.

Identify inclinations that have grown commonplace. These are matters that necessitate minimal cognitive effort on your behalf as they have been pre-programmed. Next, endeavor to identify a suitable occasion to evaluate the specific ones that could have a detrimental or unfavorable impact, and tactfully create an environment conducive to promoting more favorable daily inclinations.

Please articulate your concerns using an alternative approach

The manner in which you propose a conversation opener or address a topic plays a pivotal role in determining your response and assessing your chances of success.

Envision two specialists. One practitioner informs his patients, "The overwhelming majority of individuals who undergo this procedure survive." The other practitioner states, "A small number of individuals who undergo this technique perish."

The realities bear a striking resemblance. However, studies indicate that individuals who are presented with the statement "10% of individuals die" perceive their risk to be significantly higher.

Therefore, when faced with a decision, promptly delineate the matter. Kindly take a moment to reflect upon whether the subtle alteration in wording affects your perception of the matter.

Cease Contemplating the Issue
When one is confronted with a challenging decision, such as whether to relocate to a different city or pursue a career change, considerable time may be dedicated to contemplating the advantages and disadvantages, as well as the potential risks and rewards.

Considering that scientific research has indicated substantial value in thoughtful deliberation, excessively ruminating on decisions can pose a challenge. Assessing the advantages and disadvantages for an extended duration could potentially elevate your level of anxiety to the extent that you encounter difficulty in arriving at a decision.

Places emphasis on demonstrating the immense value derived from allowing an idea to incubate. Unconscious deliberation exhibits remarkable intelligence. Consider the possibility of deliberating upon the matter and finding solace.

Alternatively, consider immersing yourself in an activity that serves as a distraction from the matter at hand. By engaging your mind in a thorough analysis, you are more likely to develop precise and unequivocal conclusions.

One could argue that the primary observation is the absence of any certifications. No matter what actions you take, there will invariably be an element of fortuity in encountering an individual whose thoughts align suitably with your own.

However, there are a few measures you can undertake to facilitate the process of searching for that particular individual.

Reflect upon your necessities.

When embarking on the quest to witness enduring love, it is imperative to reflect upon your true desires. Occasionally, there are moments when we perceive a relationship as a potentially advantageous means to address our challenges and enhance our happiness, albeit with the acknowledgment that we remain uncertain about our desire for long-term commitment.

It may appear peculiar, nonetheless, the act of consciously choosing to seek love is, at times, a deliberate decision. It entails acknowledging that your truest requirement is something sincere and earnest, while being ready to accept all the responsibilities that may accompany it. Connections are remarkable - they have the capacity to bring immense pleasure and stability. In any event, they can also be laborious - they demand perseverance and adaptability.

It is worth considering whether you are prepared to confront both perspectives before embarking on a search for someone. By doing so, you will have the opportunity to be honest about your assumptions and expectations from the outset. You might not have complete certainty - and that is understandable. Nevertheless, making a conscious effort to anticipate your needs is preferable to proceeding without any clue whatsoever.

Reflect upon the individuals with whom you should associate

It is also highly advisable to contemplate the type of individual with whom you wish to find companionship and love. Determining our preferred choice of person may not be a straightforward task; indeed, it can often prove to be a challenge to accurately discern the type of individual we are drawn to - at times, it may even seem as if such knowledge is inherently intuitive. However, there are a few factors that ought to be taken into consideration.

Typically, individuals who align with your values tend to form meaningful and lasting connections, frequently. These deeply ingrained beliefs form the very essence of your identity, encompassing your attitudes towards work, leisure, finances, religion, family, and other

aspects of life. A sense of humor can often serve as a strong indicator of one's qualities, as our laughter often reveals our underlying beliefs and perspectives.
Formal alternative: "The presence of common interests or a shared profound interest can also yield authentic consequences. Nevertheless, in the grand scheme of things, it is often values that endure the test of time."

Endeavor to avoid being overly prescriptive
That being said, it might not be overly challenging to become excessively specific and explicit about the type of individual you are seeking. Although it is valuable to envision the kind of person who may potentially bring you fulfillment, creating a checklist of specific qualities and dismissing those who do not precisely meet it may result in denying individuals a fair opportunity.

In the era of online dating, significant emphasis is often placed on shared interests such as enjoying the same television programs, reading the same literature, and on one's physical appearance itself. In any event, there are instances where it is worthwhile to maintain an open mindset towards the type of individual with whom you might develop affinities. One might perceive this as the realization that upon gaining a deeper understanding of an individual, an additional layer of their character becomes apparent, surpassing initial perception.

Remain open to new opportunities.
Occasionally, the most efficient approach to establish connections with an individual is by encountering a multitude of unfamiliar individuals.
Creating an environment characterized by a perpetual pursuit of novel

experiences and respectful consideration of others' perspectives can heighten the possibility of cultivating a profound connection with another individual. Moreover, it has the potential to enrich various aspects of one's overall life experience. If you happen to engage in miscellaneous amusement and forge numerous new connections, it is highly likely that your self-assurance and poise will enhance. As a matter of fact, you are more inclined to become more appealing to others, irrespective of the circumstances.

It may be considered somewhat commonplace, nevertheless, I encourage you to consider joining a few social clubs that align with your interests and hobbies. You will now effectively establish a shared bond with individuals you encounter, and even if you create a deep connection with someone, you might simply forge new friendships.

Although online dating offers a remarkable avenue for connecting with individuals, it can be characterized as a rather passive process. It can also significantly emphasize the effort to meet someone with the explicit intention of initiating a relationship, thereby creating considerable tension for all parties involved. Occasionally, engaging in enjoyable activities and socializing with others can serve as a more effortless and pleasant means of establishing new connections.

4. Ensure that you have a clear understanding of your desires and expectations regarding a romantic partnership.

To mitigate the possibility of entering into an unsuitable relationship, it is imperative for individuals who are unattached to discern and ascertain the characteristics of an appropriate partnership.

I have observed that individuals desiring a committed partnership tend to select from a range of three distinct relationship styles, whether consciously or unconsciously.

The initial component would be categorized as companionship. This type of relationship may originate as a romantic relationship and gradually transition into companionship if one fails to devote attention and effort towards sustaining the romance. In this partnership, one may experience periods of solitude and ponder whether this aligns with their initial expectations.

The subsequent type of association is characterized by the bestowal of prestige. In this type of relationship, individuals are solely seeking the social dimension inherent in romantic connections. There exists a lack of affection and camaraderie, frequently giving rise to feelings of isolation.

The third category of relationship pertains to the dependency on love and intimate connection, which ultimately facilitates the achievement of happiness and contentment.

To achieve success in your romantic endeavors, it is crucial to effectively oversee the aspects that are within your sphere of influence, and the precise nature of the relationship you desire happens to be one such element. The desires and preferences of others are beyond your sphere of influence, yet by possessing a clear understanding of your own aspirations, you have the capability to draw in and discover precisely what you seek. Women who lack clarity about their desires in a romantic partnership could potentially find themselves consciously or unconsciously opting for companionship or status, ultimately leading to dissatisfaction and a sense of unmet fulfillment within their relationships.

Regrettably, I have observed this phenomenon on numerous occasions. These individuals, possessing intellect and deserving of affection, may find themselves in a predicament due to their past choices in relationships, as well as the emotional dependencies and apprehensions that can arise from being with the same person for an extended period of time. Consequently, they may endure a lifetime of discontent and lovelessness. These are the women who may exhibit signs of sadness, dissatisfaction, detachment, or in extreme cases, engage in infidelity within their relationships.

Individuals of varying age groups require affection and emotional bonds in order to cultivate a gratifying interpersonal alliance. Therefore, it would be prudent to pause and reflect upon your desires in a romantic partnership. This holds great significance for your future. It should be noted that individuals of both genders who seek a sense of fulfillment or assistance in navigating life often rely on the acquisition of social status and the presence of companionship.

Nevertheless, this seldom results in the attainment of love, contentment, and joy. If your pursuit is centered around love and connection, it is important to bear that in mind and actively seek those aspects in a deliberate manner within your subsequent relationship.

Do not assume that every gentleman who takes an interest in your personage harbors identical intentions as your own. Do not rely on chance. It is imperative to establish a clear understanding within oneself and communicate with potential partners about one's romantic and life aspirations.

What qualities and attributes do you seek in a potential partner?

In order to discover love, establish meaningful connections, and attain fulfillment within a relationship, it is essential to possess a clear understanding of the specific qualities and attributes you desire in a partner, and refrain from accepting anything that falls below your established standards. However, it is imperative that you first comprehend your established criteria.

Your standards represent the fundamental principles that guide you. They are present to establish boundaries for your actions, convictions, cognitions, inclinations, or predilections. They ultimately contribute to shaping your identity. We all possess standards, whether they are consciously acknowledged or not.

In order to experience happiness and a sense of fulfillment, it is imperative that one attains their standards or prerequisites. They inevitably and implicitly constitute your priorities, regardless of your level of consciousness about them.

The determination of one's necessities or criteria is contingent upon multiple factors, including physical, emotional, cultural, and social circumstances, as well as individual disposition.

Regardless of the intensity of a man's infatuation or the enchantment he may fall under, it is inconsequential. "No matter to what extent a man may be infatuated and enamored with you, or whatever enchantment you may cast upon him, it holds no significance." If he does not incite a fluttering sensation in your stomach or elicit excitement every time his voice reaches your ears, it is unlikely that he will bring you complete happiness and contentment. Ultimately, it is solely your prerogative to determine this.

Occasionally, cultivating such emotions for a gentleman may require a certain amount of time, yet once they are fully realized, it becomes evident that he is the indivisible choice.

Should you find yourself after a period of time questioning whether or not he sincerely fulfills your desired criteria, or if you experience hesitancy concerning your emotions towards him, it is likely that these sensations serve as indications from your genuine inner being. It is imperative that you avoid discontinuing their access.

There exist numerous distinguished gentlemen in society, although not all possess the qualities that align with your personal preferences and compatibility. It is imperative that you possess unwavering certainty in your belief that he is the individual destined for you, and be captivated by one or more of his qualities, be it his persona, articulation, manner of treating you, or any alluring aspect that exerts an undeniable attraction upon you.

Do not deceive yourself into believing that the passage of time will bring about a miraculous occurrence, causing you to develop an intense attraction towards him.

The construction of this indomitable magnet cannot be achieved through the investment of either time or exertion.

In a relationship lacking in an irresistible allure, it is highly probable that over time, a profound sense of admiration for one another and immense satisfaction will flourish. However, numerous women whom I have encountered in such relationships have expressed to me a sense of incompleteness, despite leading what appears to be a contented life.

Despite years of being in a committed relationship with their amiable partners, they yearn for the ardor, enchantment, and allure that they have never truly experienced with the individual they have chosen to spend their lives with. They do not experience complete contentment if they choose to remain in a relationship that does not genuinely fulfill them. Regrettably, they ultimately compromise, accepting outcomes that are below their desired levels and rightful expectations.

Establish Your Criteria for a Relationship

To ascertain your relationship criteria, it is imperative to have a lucid comprehension of your fundamental principles and beliefs. Your standards encompass the qualities in an individual that align with your personal values, aspirations, and ambitions. To experience a sense of fulfillment, one must ensure that their standards are congruent with their personal identity and aspirations.

To ascertain your standards, it is advisable to introspect and determine whether they are necessary for your happiness and sense of security within a relationship. If the response entails that I do not require certain factors to experience happiness and security in a relationship, it becomes evident that this deviates from the norm.

It is imperative that you engage in the straightforward activity titled "what you give is what you get."

Initially, compile a comprehensive enumeration of the attributes defining your ideal male counterpart. This compilation embodies the qualities and characteristics that are desirable in a gentleman. Please jot down the attributes and qualities that epitomize him as your ideal partner. Subsequently, it is necessary to categorize the list into two distinct classifications.

The initial category comprises the essential or standard requirements, while the subsequent category pertains to the desirable or optional features.

The criteria encompassing both essentials and desirable qualities may encompass his appearance, emotional well-being, societal standing, intellectual aptitude, benevolence, or any other factors of significance to you. The utmost significance of this exercise lies in attaining a lucid understanding of which elements within the list encompass your established benchmarks.

The next step, after establishing a clear understanding of your expectations and non-negotiable traits in a potential partner, is to introspect and evaluate if you possess corresponding qualities.

When engaging in this exercise, it is opportune to engage in self-reflection and identify areas for personal growth, as well as determine the actionable steps necessary to attain such advancement.

This activity has proven transformative for numerous women, enabling them to embrace their individual ideals and enhance their personal growth. Their motivation does not stem from a desire to emulate others, but rather from an awakening to their untapped potential.

This activity has the potential to provide a sense of lucidity regarding areas requiring enhancement in order for individuals to experience optimal well-being. It is not necessary for you to achieve perfection. Simply align yourself with your own set of standards.

This exercise will assist you in recognizing that it is unreasonable to expect a man to possess something that you yourself do not already have. While one may hold the expectation or desire for such qualities, making them a non-negotiable criterion or a requisite in a man sets a significant distinction.

If, for instance, a criterion for you in assessing a man is his adherence to a healthy lifestyle, it follows that you must also abide by a healthy lifestyle. This now becomes an essential criterion for your prospective partner. Indeed, it is impossible to expect an individual to embody characteristics that do not align with their own nature.

Should you happen to discover that a gentleman who maintains a healthy lifestyle is a desirable attribute, but it is of no concern to you if he does not adhere to such a lifestyle, it is not obligatory for you to adopt a similar lifestyle in order to find your ideal partner.

The so-called "nice to haves" encompass all other attributes or qualities that one values in a partner, yet they are deemed non-essential for experiencing contentment and fulfillment within a relationship.

This exercise affords the opportunity to discern essential qualities in a partner or factors that are sought after in a partner. Although there are countless possibilities, undertaking this exercise will lead you to discern that the fundamental qualities you desire in a companion can be succinctly encapsulated.

Within the segment titled "Discerning a Victorious Individual and Negating the Fallacy of Victory," you shall acquire knowledge regarding the essential attributes a companion must possess in order for you to attain the desired state of contentment and affectionate companionship.

Attracting Your Ideal Relationship

Step #1

It is now the appropriate moment to engage in enjoyable activities. Prior to proceeding, I kindly request that you articulate a comprehensive narrative outlining your envisioned parameters for an ideal interpersonal bond. Craft a narrative or composition, tailored precisely to your desires and specifications. Exhibit your creativity without constraints, the possibilities are boundless. Engage in a thorough exploration of articulating your ideal relationship, enabling yourself to evoke the tactile sensation associated with experiencing such a relationship. We will discuss your envisioned gentleman in the subsequent section.

May I inquire about your place of residence, the architectural style of your dwelling, the interior furnishings, the routine of your daily life, the nature of your social engagements, your shared and individual activities, the role of travel in your ideal relationship, the dynamics of your familial interactions, your engagement with your profession, and the allocation of time spent together and apart? Ensure that your description is highly comprehensive.

Cease your current activities and proceed to compose a detailed account detailing the nature and characteristics of your envisioned ideal romantic partnership at this moment.

Now, I kindly request that you carefully observe the aforementioned description and proceed to extract each distinct element that has been described. Subsequently, I would appreciate it if you would transcribe these individual elements, in the form of a list, within the pages of your journal. Please ensure that there is adequate spacing after each item.

The subsequent course of action involves addressing the question of "why." What are the underlying motivations behind desiring each of these components that you have outlined as integral to your ideal relationship? Inquiring about the reasoning behind something is consistently an illuminating endeavor. Engaging in this activity will provide you with valuable insights into your own being. I would advise you to engage in this procedure subsequent to a session of Relaxation Meditation to facilitate a deeper introspection, enabling you to connect with your genuine truths.

Cease and articulate the reasoning behind your desire for each item enlisted in your journal.

Now, proceed to articulate the anticipated emotional experience associated with each listed item.

• Cease your actions momentarily and articulate the anticipated sensation associated with every item on your inventory.

Step #2

What you have elucidated embodies the epitome of a conceivable ideal relationship. Moving forward, I shall assist you in further refining it.

To further enhance your clarity and consequently, draw towards you that which you truly desire, consider posing the subsequent inquiry to yourself: What is the underlying reason for my desire to be in a romantic partnership?

This query may appear self-evident or trivial in nature. However, upon careful contemplation, it will afford you a more lucid understanding of your desired objectives. Naturally, there are the primary reasons:

- You desire to enter into the institution of marriage.
- You desire to have children.
- You desire a long-term companion to age alongside
- You seek a lifelong partner to share your life's journey with
- You long for a companion to spend your golden years with
- You yearn for a lifelong confidant to accompany you through the aging process.

- You seek a partner to share sexual pleasure with
- You desire companionship for sexual fulfillment
- You are in search of a compatible individual to engage in a pleasurable sexual experience with
- You long for a

suitable companion for a mutually enjoyable sexual encounter
• You desire a companion to accompany you in your life journey.
• You desire membership within a united community.
• You are seeking financial stability
• You desire the presence of a companion during the night.
• You have grown weary of solitude • You are fatigued by your lack of companionship • You are longing for the presence of others • You are seeking respite from the burden of isolation.

• Please record your responses in your personal journal.
All of those reasons mentioned are valid and justifiable motives for desiring to be in a romantic partnership. In fact, they are the very elements that most women desire.
However, I urge you to delve into the core of your true desires. In order to achieve that, it is necessary to delve beyond superficial appearances and

explore the profound desires that reside within the innermost recesses of your being. That is where the underlying causes are situated. In order to ascertain the genuine truth about oneself, as well as one's desires, beliefs, and values, it is crucial to pose the fundamental query: What is the underlying motivation for these aspirations?

If the rationale behind your desire to engage in a romantic partnership is rooted in your aspiration for matrimony, it would be prudent to introspect on the underlying motivation. If you desire to find a lifelong companion, inquire into the reasons behind it. When expressing a desire, regardless of its nature, it is advisable to introspect and ascertain the underlying motivation behind it. This introspective process will facilitate a better understanding of your genuine aspirations, leading you closer to your most profound yearnings.

When confronted with the necessity of making a decision, inquire within yourself as to the underlying reasons, so as to discern the profound truth that motivates your actions. This can prove to be more challenging to access than one might initially assume. I would recommend engaging in a relaxation meditation practice in order to achieve a state of tranquility and calmness within your consciousness. This represents the sole method through which you can apprehend the messages your subconscious desires to convey to you.

To engage in this relaxation meditation, assume a seated position in a chair, ensuring that the ambient lighting is diminished. Select a moment during which you can expect minimal interference from telephones, young ones, or any other disruptions. Please make yourself comfortable, gently close your eyes, take a few deliberate and deep breaths, and as you exhale, allow your body to enter a state of relaxation. Conduct a comprehensive assessment of each muscle group within your body, commencing from your toes and progressing towards the crown of your head, in order to alleviate any accumulated tension.

Once you have achieved a state of complete relaxation, kindly request the assistance of your Inner Wise Self. This artwork serves as a manifestation of your authentic essence, your innate discernment, and your profound wisdom, encapsulating the facet within you that possesses profound awareness of your genuine truth at the very core of your being. If you are able to conceive of an image that symbolizes this aspect of your identity, it would be even more advantageous. It could assume the form of an illumination, an individual, or a botanical entity, without distinction. It is merely an aid for directing one's attention towards detaching from the external world.

After achieving a state of relaxation, kindly inquire as follows:

What are the underlying reasons behind my desire to enter into a romantic partnership? (It may be beneficial to prompt yourself with the following: I desire a romantic partnership because... and subsequently provide an answer.)

If one exercises patience, solutions will gradually manifest themselves, akin to a gentle whisper. Please ensure that your journal is within reach, and proceed to write down any thoughts or ideas that arise. Refrain from making any modifications, refrain from experiencing shock, and simply permit your internal wisdom to educate you about your own being.

Herein lie a few illustrative instances of the prospective discoveries you might encounter regarding your own persona.

"I desire to engage in a romantic partnership due to the following reasons:

I no longer desire to experience solitude.
• I require affection.
I require to be valued and treasured.
• I deeply appreciate the sensation of being embraced by a gentleman who harbors genuine affection for me.
• I have concerns about facing old age without a partner or companionship.

I possess a considerable amount of affection to offer, and I am in search of a companion with whom I can share this abundance.

I feel a deep sense of embarrassment that I have not yet entered into matrimony.

- I strongly dislike being the sole unmarried individual within my social circle.
- The absence of children would leave me with a sense of unfulfillment in my life.

I find it burdensome to constantly have to coordinate plans for watching a movie or dining outside.

- I aspire to embark on a global exploration and seek to undertake this remarkable adventure alongside my beloved husband.

I aspire to demonstrate to both myself and my family that I possess the capability to surpass my previous marital experience.

- What factors have you identified as the underlying motivations behind your desire to pursue a romantic relationship? Record them in your personal journal.

I strongly urge you to engage in extensive introspection, as it is within this process that valuable insights can be discovered. As you delve deeper, your understanding and consciousness will be further enriched. By cultivating awareness, you will gain greater agency in shaping the course of your life. In the absence of consciousness, meaningful change seldom transpires, and when it does, it transpires fortuitously and evades your jurisdiction.

In order for your life to undergo significant improvement, it is imperative that you contemplate making alterations and take the initiative to actively shape the direction of those modifications. If you persist with your current course, the circumstances will remain unchanged, consistent with their past state.

If your genuine intention is to allure the most suitable partner for yourself, while simultaneously enhancing your interpersonal connections, delving deeper into the essence of your true self through inquiring 'why' is undeniably the apt course of action.

For Each response you generate, it would be prudent to inquire, "What is the underlying motive behind such a desire?" The interrogative 'Why' consistently penetrates the profoundest depths of your essence. Continuously inquire 'why' at each successive stage, until you reach the very core of your personal truth. This process exudes a significant degree of self-revelation and holds the potential to expedite the manifestation of the desired trajectory of your life.

Once you are able to ascertain the fundamental reason behind your pursuit, you will move significantly nearer to attracting a suitable partner for yourself. How will you recognize the moment when you have attained your most profound authenticity? You will discern it through instinctual feeling. You possess the knowledge of the answers; you are merely divulging the veracity.

During the course of engaging in this inquiry that delves into progressively profound layers of causation, it is plausible that a portion of the knowledge you acquire may elicit distressing emotional responses. That's okay. Removing those impediments, eliminating any obstacles that have hindered you from attaining the desired companionship, will pave the way for fostering genuine love. It is not to be evaded or feared.

Each of us possesses matters that we prefer to overlook. However, by extracting these emotions and addressing them, you will be able to cultivate a more receptive and generous disposition towards both receiving and offering love. At that moment, an exceptional gentleman will be inclined towards your affectionate aura, perceiving your authentic essence and admiring the profound elegance of your soul.

The most recent encounter I had with my father occurred when I was three years old. He made two phone calls during my adulthood; aside from those instances, I have lived my entire life without the presence of a father. The rationales behind my desire for a partner, the culmination of introspecting upon my multifaceted motivations, will inevitably be influenced by this pertinent aspect. They will exhibit dissimilar qualities compared to a woman who had the privilege of an affectionate father during her upbringing. Your motivations are distinctive and personal, contributing to your individuality and shaping your identity. It constitutes an integral piece within the tapestry of one's life, and as we gain a deeper comprehension of our own identity, remarkable opportunities commence to manifest in our existence.

Treating Yourself Right

How one conducts themselves will establish the precedent for how others should treat them.
~ Marrilyn Soo Hui Tong

I experienced a profoundly distressing dissolution of a previous romantic bond, preceding my present relationship, which instilled within me a profound sense of wrath. I held a profound disdain for my former romantic partner. Our relationship had a tumultuous end, and compounding the situation was his inappropriate advances towards one of my acquaintances. On the day of my departure, he extended an invitation to her to the shared apartment we resided in.

He would implore me for financial assistance, asserting that he required it for sustenance; he would even solicit monetary funds to partake in outings with her. It goes without saying that I was deeply distraught. By the conclusion of the third and fourth week, I experienced a complete breakdown. I recall experiencing a loss of self-control while seated in the rear of a taxi; I commenced uttering explicit, uncontrolled remarks directed towards the cab driver. The taxi driver perhaps perceived me as mentally unbalanced. I, too, had the impression that my sanity was slipping away. That was a catalyzing moment! I recognized it was imperative to promptly take action in order to alter my circumstances.

I initiated the implementation of the exercises delineated in the preceding . They contribute to my overall well-being and enhance my self-esteem. I undertook an extensive endeavor to thoroughly clean and organize my room, subsequently opting to indulge in self-care. I began frequenting a café that I had occasionally patronized before, and in doing so, I cultivated new acquaintances. Subsequently, I discovered that they were commencing a Kundalini Yoga class, a practice I had longed to experience but had not yet been afforded the opportunity to do so. I seized the opportunity with enthusiasm and expressed gratitude to the Universe for its fortuitous timing. I commenced my participation in the yoga lessons, fortuitously discovering that the instructor was delivering exercises designed to facilitate the release and elimination of superfluous past baggage, along with the negativity entrenched within oneself. I am astounded by the profound sense of cosmic alignment that seemed to orchestrate every minute detail, leading to an unmistakable state of bliss, subsequent to my deliberate choice to pursue happiness.

I initiated a process of self-indulgence by acquiring floral arrangements and exhibiting them in my living quarters. Pursuing regular massage and facial treatments while enrolling in a fitness center to achieve weight loss goals and enhance my self-confidence. All of these experiences contributed to an increased sense of self-fulfillment, serving as demonstrations of practicing self-care and self-worth.

Instead of socializing with my usual companions, I spent time with unfamiliar individuals. I initiated a romantic relationship mere weeks after implementing my resolution to alter the existing state of affairs. If my memory serves me correctly, I indeed accompanied four gentlemen, some of whom I held quite a strong affection for, while the rest were purely platonic companions. Despite not entering official relationships with any of them, I have maintained a strong and lasting friendship with one individual up to the present day.

I am genuinely appreciative of the opportunity that facilitated my encounter with these remarkable individuals. Therefore, would you be able to perceive this as one opportunity closing while another presents itself? We are all fated to undergo numerous experiences. Individuals enter and exit our lives with purpose, necessitating our trust in the workings of the Universe, our esteemed guide. Through her teachings, I was able to journey from profound desolation to a joyous existence, leading to the formation of new friendships and the prospect of romantic relationships, all within the span of a brief three weeks. In addition, she will provide assistance to you, but it is essential for you to be ready to invest effort in personal growth, as I have done. Taking proper care of oneself is the individual obligation associated with adulthood. We uphold our well-being by assuming the roles of responsible guardians towards ourselves.

The individuals who possess a compassionate and empathetic nature often display a tendency to prioritize the well-being of others over their own, exhibiting a nurturing disposition. You have successfully attended to the needs of everyone else, with the exception of a single individual — yourself!

While it is paramount to consistently exhibit kindness towards others, it is equally imperative that we acquire the ability to enhance our self-care practices and lead a more fulfilling existence. When we prioritize our own well-being, it will have a beneficial effect on those in our proximity as well.

If you have recently experienced a romantic separation or the bereavement of a cherished individual, it is imperative that you avoid indulging in excessive self-pity and instead seek ways to move forward. Allow yourself a designated period of time, as you are deserving of it, to embrace feelings of melancholy, and indeed, it is imperative that you do so! By fully immersing yourself in the depths of your sorrow, rage, or distress, you shall discover that it will ultimately dissipate. "I would like to draw your attention to a proverbial expression that I believe warrants contemplation:

What one opposes or resists, has a tendency to persist.

What this implies is that in the event of your WILLINGNESS to refrain from suppressing the tears, inhibiting the expression of words (such as in the taxi cab scenario), or resisting the engulfment of sadness. . . then it will PERSIST!

Take a vow to prioritize self-care on this day.

~ Exercise ~

Identify an activity that you have long desired to undertake but previously lacked the opportunity to pursue, and proceed to engage in said endeavor. One may engage in activities such as writing, enrolling in a dance class, vocalizing, or participating in various forms of physical exercise.

Compile a comprehensive inventory of actions you can undertake to commence the process of nurturing and cherishing oneself, while cultivating a sense of self-romance.

Commence by introspecting, "If I aspire to prioritize self-care, what measures shall I take?" and "What actions can be undertaken to foster a sense of self-indulgence?"

A reliable metric would be to select a minimum of five activities to engage in. The more the merrier.

You may require additional time to commence the activities you intend to pursue within this particular domain. It is possible that you may be interested in locating a yoga class, which is scheduled to commence a week from now. This is ok. There is an absence of a predetermined timeframe for this exercise; however, it is imperative that you diligently engage in the assigned tasks.

Please set aside this book for now and resume reading the following section tomorrow.

www.ingramcontent.com/pod-product-compliance
Lightning Source LLC
Chambersburg PA
CBHW050420120526
44590CB00015B/2038